Francis Frith's
Scotland

Photographic Memories

Francis Frith's
Scotland

Clive Hardy

First published in the United Kingdom in 1998
by WBC Ltd

Revised Paperback Edition published in the United Kingdom in 2000
by Frith Book Company Ltd
ISBN 1-85937-182-5

Reprinted in Paperback 2003

Francis Frith's Scotland
Clive Hardy

Frith Book Company Ltd
Frith's Barn, Teffont,
Salisbury, Wiltshire SP3 5QP
Tel: +44 (0) 1722 716 376
Email: info@francisfrith.co.uk
www.francisfrith.co.uk

Printed and bound in Great Britain

Front Cover: **Perth, High Street West 1899** 43900

The colour-tinting is for illustrative purposes only, and is not intended to be historically accurate

Contents

Francis Frith: *Victorian Pioneer*

FRANCIS FRITH, Victorian founder of the world-famous photographic archive, was a complex and multitudinous man. A devout Quaker and a highly successful Victorian businessman, he was both philosophic by nature and pioneering in outlook.

By 1855 Francis Frith had already established a wholesale grocery business in Liverpool, and sold it for the astonishing sum of £200,000, which is the equivalent today of over £15,000,000. Now a very rich man, he was able to indulge his passion for travel. As a child he had pored over travel books written by early explorers, and his fancy and imagination had been stirred by family holidays to the sublime mountain regions of Wales and Scotland. 'What a land of spirit-stirring and enriching scenes and places!' he had written. He was to return to these scenes of grandeur in later years to 'recapture the thousands of vivid and tender memories', but with a different purpose. Now in his thirties, and captivated by the new science of photography, Frith set out on a series of pioneering journeys to the Nile regions that occupied him from 1856 until 1860.

Intrigue and Adventure

He took with him on his travels a specially-designed wicker carriage that acted as both dark-room and sleeping chamber. These far-flung journeys were packed with intrigue and adventure. In his life story, written when he was sixty-three, Frith tells of being held captive by bandits, and of fighting 'an awful midnight battle to the very point of surrender with a deadly pack of hungry, wild dogs'. Sporting flowing Arab costume, Frith arrived at Akaba by camel seventy years before Lawrence, where he encountered 'desert princes and rival sheikhs, blazing with jewel-hilted swords'.

During these extraordinary adventures he was assiduously exploring the desert regions bordering the Nile and patiently recording the antiquities and peoples with his camera. He was the first photographer to venture beyond the sixth cataract. Africa was still the mysterious 'Dark Continent', and Stanley and Livingstone's historic meeting was a decade into the future. The conditions for picture taking confound belief. He laboured for hours in his wicker dark-room in the sweltering heat of the desert, while the volatile chemicals fizzed dangerously in their trays. Often he was forced to work in remote tombs and caves where conditions were cooler. Back in London he exhibited his photographs and

was 'rapturously cheered' by members of the Royal Society. His reputation as a photographer was made overnight. An eminent modern historian has likened their impact on the population of the time to that on our own generation of the first photographs taken on the surface of the moon.

Venture of a Life-Time

Characteristically, Frith quickly spotted the opportunity to create a new business as a specialist publisher of photographs. He lived in an era of immense and sometimes violent change. For the poor in the early part of Victoria's reign work was a drudge and the hours long, and people had precious little free time to enjoy themselves. Most had no transport other than a cart or gig at their disposal, and had not travelled far beyond the

boundaries of their own town or village. However, by the 1870s, the railways had threaded their way across the country, and Bank Holidays and half-day Saturdays had been made obligatory by Act of Parliament. All of a sudden the ordinary working man and his family were able to enjoy days out and see a little more of the world.

With characteristic business acumen, Francis Frith foresaw that these new tourists would enjoy having souvenirs to commemorate their days out. In 1860 he married Mary Ann Rosling and set out with the intention of photographing every city, town and village in Britain. For the next thirty years he travelled the country by train and by pony and trap, producing fine photographs of seaside resorts and beauty spots that were keenly bought by millions of Victorians. These prints were painstakingly pasted into family albums and pored over during the dark nights of winter, rekindling precious memories of summer excursions.

The Rise of Frith & Co

Frith's studio was soon supplying retail shops all over the country. To meet the demand he gathered about him a small team of photographers, and published the work of independent artist-photographers of the calibre of Roger Fenton and Francis Bedford. In order to gain some understanding of the scale of Frith's business one only has to look at the catalogue issued by Frith & Co in 1886: it runs to some 670 pages, listing not only many thousands of views of the British Isles but also many photographs of most European countries, and China, Japan, the USA and

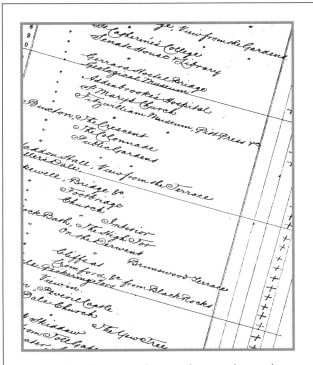

Canada – note the sample page shown above from the hand-written *Frith & Co* ledgers detailing pictures taken. By 1890 Frith had created the greatest specialist photographic publishing company in the world, with over 2,000 outlets – more than the combined number that Boots and WH Smith have today! The picture on the right shows the *Frith & Co* display board at Ingleton in the Yorkshire Dales (left of window). Beautifully constructed with a mahogany frame and gilt inserts, it could display up to a dozen local scenes.

Postcard Bonanza

The ever-popular holiday postcard we know today took many years to develop. In 1870 the Post Office issued the first plain cards, with a pre-printed stamp on one face. In 1894 they allowed other publishers' cards to be sent through the mail with an attached adhesive halfpenny stamp. Demand grew rapidly, and

in 1895 a new size of postcard was permitted called the court card, but there was little room for illustration. In 1899, a year after Frith's death, a new card measuring 5.5 x 3.5 inches became the standard format, but it was not until 1902 that the divided back came into being, with address and message on one face and a full-size illustration on the other. *Frith & Co* were in the vanguard of postcard development, and Frith's sons Eustace and Cyril continued their father's monumental task, expanding the number of views offered to the public and recording more and more places in Britain, as the coasts and countryside were opened up to mass travel.

Francis Frith died in 1898 at his villa in Cannes, his great project still growing. The archive he created continued in business for another seventy years. By 1970 it contained over a third of a million pictures of 7,000 cities, towns and villages. The massive photographic record Frith has left to us stands as a living monument to a special and very remarkable man.

Frith's Archive: *A Unique Legacy*

FRANCIS FRITH'S legacy to us today is of immense significance and value, for the magnificent archive of evocative photographs he created provides a unique record of change in 7,000 cities, towns and villages throughout Britain over a century and more. Frith and his fellow studio photographers revisited locations many times down the years to update their views, compiling for us an enthralling and colourful pageant of British life and character.

We tend to think of Frith's sepia views of Britain as nostalgic, for most of us use them to conjure up memories of places in our own lives with which we have family associations. It often makes us forget that to Francis Frith they were records of daily life as it was actually being lived in the cities, towns and villages of his day. The Victorian age was one of great and often bewildering change for ordinary people, and though the pictures evoke an impression of slower times, life was as busy and hectic as it is today.

We are fortunate that Frith was a photographer of the people, dedicated to recording the minutiae of everyday life. For it is this sheer wealth of visual data, the painstaking chronicle of changes in dress, transport, street layouts, buildings, housing, engineering and landscape that captivates us so much today. His remarkable images offer us a powerful link with the past and with the lives of our ancestors.

Today's Technology

Computers have now made it possible for Frith's many thousands of images to be accessed almost instantly. In the Frith archive today, each photograph is carefully 'digitised' then stored on a CD Rom. Frith archivists can locate a single photograph amongst thousands within seconds. Views can be catalogued and sorted under a variety of categories of place and content to the immediate benefit of researchers.

Inexpensive reference prints can be created for them at the touch of a mouse button, and a wide range of books and other printed materials assembled and published for a wider, more general readership. The day-to-day workings of the archive are very different from how they were in Francis Frith's time: imagine the herculean task of sorting through eleven tons of glass negatives as Frith had to do to locate a particular sequence of pictures! Yet the archive still prides itself on maintaining the same high

See Frith at www.francisfrith.co.uk

standards of excellence laid down by Francis Frith, including the painstaking cataloguing and indexing of every view.

It is curious to reflect on how the internet now allows researchers in America and elsewhere greater instant access to the archive than Frith himself ever enjoyed. Many thousands of individual views can be called up on screen within seconds on one of the Frith internet sites, enabling people living continents away to revisit the streets of their ancestral home town, or view places in Britain where they have enjoyed holidays. Many overseas researchers welcome the chance to view special theme selections, such as transport, sports, costume and ancient monuments.

We are certain that Francis Frith would have heartily approved of these modern developments in imaging techniques, for he himself was always working at the very limits of Victorian photographic technology.

The Value of the Archive Today

Because of the benefits brought by the computer, Frith's images are increasingly studied by social historians, by researchers into genealogy and ancestory, by architects, town planners, and by teachers and schoolchildren involved in local history projects.

In addition, the archive offers every one of us an opportunity to examine the places where we and our families have lived and worked down the years. Highly successful in Frith's own era, the archive is now, a century and more on, entering a new phase of popularity.

The Past in Tune with the Future

Historians consider the Francis Frith Collection to be of prime national importance. It is the only archive of its kind remaining in private ownership and has been valued at a million pounds. However, this figure is now rapidly increasing as digital technology enables more and more people around the world to enjoy its benefits.

Francis Frith's archive is now housed in an historic timber barn in the beautiful village of Teffont in Wiltshire. Its founder would not recognize the archive office as it is today. In place of the many thousands of dusty boxes containing glass plate negatives and an all-pervading odour of photographic chemicals, there are now ranks of computer screens. He would be amazed to watch his images travelling round the world at unimaginable speeds through network and internet lines.

The archive's future is both bright and exciting. Francis Frith, with his unshakeable belief in making photographs available to the greatest number of people, would undoubtedly approve of what is being done today with his lifetime's work. His photographs, depicting our shared past, are now bringing pleasure and enlightenment to millions around the world a century and more after his death.

Dumfries and Galloway

Moffat, A Tennis Tournament 1892 M113003
At the beginning of the 20th century, Moffat attracted tourists wishing to sample the delights of the nearby sulphureous-saline wells. It was around this time that tennis became something of an event, with most spa towns starting to hold annual tournaments.

◄ **Gretna
Sark Bridge c1955**
G163014
Gretna stands on the Scottish/English border, and so it became popular for runaway marriages of English couples following the passage of Lord Hardwicke's act in 1754. The act abolished irregular marriages in England but not Scotland. Once across the bridge, runaways from England could be married very quickly in accordance with 18th-century Scots law, which required neither banns nor a licence.

Moffat, High Street
1890 M113002
At this time Moffat was one of Scotland's chief inland resorts, boasting several hotels, a hydropathic establishment and private boarding houses. During the season the town's population of just more than 2,000 would more than double.

Gretna, The Blacksmith's Shop
c1955 G163009
From 1826 this shop became the most popular place in Gretna for declaratory marriages. After 1856, a residence north of the border of not less than three weeks was required before a marriage could take place.

Gretna
The Interior Of The Smithy c1955 G163008
Marriages also took place at Gretna Hall and at the Toll Inn and the Sark Toll Bar.

Dumfries
The Bridges c1890
D78002
The River Nith divides
Dumfries from
Maxwelltown. Dumfries
itself became a royal
burgh in the 12th
century, but the two
towns were not officially
amalgamated until
1929. Robert Burns
came to the town in
1791 and lived with his
wife and family in a
house in Millhole Brae.
Burns died in 1796 at
the age of 36 and is
buried in St Michael's
Church. It was here, in
February 1306, that
Robert Bruce killed John
Comyn the Red. Five
weeks later, Bruce was
crowned king of
Scotland.

Strathclyde

Glasgow

The Act of Union that joined Scotland with England established Glasgow's potential as a port and industrial centre. Glasgow was ideally situated to take advantage of the trade with the American colonies. American requirements for textiles, for instance, transformed Scotland's linen industry to such an extent that by 1778 there were 4,000 handlooms in Glasgow alone. After the American War of Independence, the price of flax rocketed and cotton was looked upon as a viable alternative. By 1787, no fewer than nineteen cotton mills were at work, rising to over 200 within a few decades.

In the 1750s, English iron founders discovered that it was cheaper to ship ore to Scotland for smelting due to the availability of cheap charcoal. However, it was the discovery in the early 1800s of a local source of top quality ironstone that gave the industry a much needed boost. By 1847, Scotland was producing 25 per cent of Britain's iron. During the late 17th century other businesses were established, including a soap works using whale blubber, a sugar refinery, a rope-works and a glass-works. There were also several candle factories and a number of coal-pits.

It was the advent of steam-power that saw the development of Glasgow's two greatest industries - shipbuilding and railway locomotives. The ship-yards included John Brown & Co. of Clydebank, A & J Inglis Ltd and D & W Henderson & Co. Railway locomotives were manufactured by the North British Locomotive Co, an amalgamation of three companies employing 7,000 workers. In total, the NBL built about 20,000 railway locomotives for customers world-wide.

Glasgow, Buchanan Street 1897 39767
This was one of the busiest thoroughfares in the city. At one end was the Caledonian Railway station, where trains could be caught for Oban, Perth and the north; at the other was St Enoch Station. Buchanan Street was a great place to eat out, with several top restaurants including Queen's at number 70 and Ferguson & Forrester at number 36.

Glasgow, Argyle Street 1897 39765
In late Victorian Glasgow, Argyle Street, Buchanan Street, Union Street and Sauchiehall Street were considered the places for shopping.

Glasgow, Renfield Street 1897 39769
A convoy of horse-trams trundle along Renfield Street. Within a year, electric street trams would be running, and the horse-trams were phased out. Glasgow was the last city in the UK to abandon its tramway system. The Leeds system closed in 1959, Sheffield in 1960 and Glasgow in 1962.

Glasgow, St Vincent's Place 1897 39764
St Vincent's Place was right in the commercial heart of the city with the National Bank, the Royal Exchange, the Stock Exchange, and the Athenaeum club all nearby. This view looks towards George Square.

Glasgow, Sauchiehall Street 1897 39763
Joining the east and west quarters of the city, this was where you could buy quality confectionery from Assafrey, dine out at the Hippodrome, attend an exhibition at the Institute of Fine Arts, or stay at a temperance hotel.

**Glasgow
George Square 1897**
39759
It used to be said that George Square reminded visiting Londoners of Trafalgar Square, but the central column was a monument to Sir Walter Scott rather than Lord Nelson. The square served to emphasise Glasgow's self-proclaimed status as 'the second city of the Empire'. It contained the magnificent municipal buildings completed in 1888 at a cost of £540,000 - the post office, the Bank of Scotland, the Merchant's House and several hotels.

▼ Glasgow, The Grand Hotel 1897 39768

The Grand Hotel at the west end of Charing Cross had rooms from 3s 6d a night, with dinner costing 5s. The two most expensive hotels were the Central and the Windsor, where rooms started at 4s 6d a night. Most hotels charged around 5s for dinner, although the Victoria in West George Street charged just 3s 6d.

▼ Glasgow, The Cathedral 1890 G11001

The Cathedral stands on the site of an earlier building destroyed by fire in 1192. The choir and tower date from the 13th century, and the spire was added about two centuries later. The tower is 220 ft high. Behind the cathedral is the Necropolis, which contains a number of substantial monuments to the great and the good as well as to those who had enough money to make sure that when they were gone, they would not be forgotten.

▲ Glasgow Broomielaw 1897 39801
This overhead view of the Broomielaw area of the city shows the George V bridge in the foreground. Ships are tied up at the quay waiting to load up with cargo and passengers for the Clyde and Scottish coastal resorts.

15

16

**◄ Glasgow
The Botanic Gardens
1897** 39795
The Botanic Gardens are situated off Great Western Road. Many rare orchids, tree ferns and other plants grow here, including bananas. The Kibble Palace is the largest glasshouse in Britain.

**Glasgow
Kelvingrove Park
1897** 39757
The central feature here is the Stewart memorial fountain. The park was chosen as the site for a museum and art gallery, which opened in 1901. For decades, the art gallery contained the finest municipal collection of Dutch, French and Scottish schools in Britain.

Bothwell, The Castle 1897 39867

Three hundred years ago, Bothwell was a strategically important village, its bridge being the only one over the Clyde apart from Glasgow Bridge. In 1679, the Duke of Monmouth defeated the Covenanters at the Battle of Bothwell Brig. Dating back to the 13th century, the castle is one of the most impressive ruined fortresses in Scotland; the Douglas Tower took 36 years to build, and is thought to be the work of French masons because it resembles a similar structure at Coucy in France.

Paisley, High Street 1900 45993

Although spinning and weaving were Paisley's main industries, there were also several shipyards along the banks of the River Cart. The longest lived was Fleming & Ferguson. There was also the Thistle shipyard, which closed in the 1930s but was reopened during the Second World War for the construction of landing craft. Note the different styles of street lights in this view. There are at least three on the right-hand side, and on the left the remains of gaslights are very much in evidence.

Paisley, Dunn Square 1901 47397

By 1900, Paisley was a smoky industrial town with a population of 80,000. Paisley was the last stronghold of the highly skilled craft of fine handloom weaving, and as late as 1834 there were few if any power looms in the town. The Paisley weavers were specialists, producing goods for a luxury market. The end came not so much from power looms, but from printed imitations. In one Glasgow mill they used a treadmill worked by a Newfoundland dog.

Paisley, Dunn Square 1897 39802

In 1906, Paisley was described as a 'smoke-begrimed industrial town on the Cart with 79,355 inhabitants and large thread, shawl and corn-flour factories'. Coats & Clark manufactured thread, and Brown & Poulson corn-flour.

Kilbarchan
Main Street 1884
K108001
In the mid 18th century, the town was noted for weaving: there were more than 1,000 hand-looms in operation in the area. On the steeple of the church is a statue of Habbie Simpson, a well-known piper of the late 16th century.

◄ **Greenock**
Union Street 1899 43405
One of the most famous shipyards was that of John Scott, which built the first steamer to trade between Glasgow and Liverpool. The East India Harbour was completed in 1806-07, the Victoria Dock opened during the 1850s and the Albert Dock followed a decade or so later. Greenock was the birthplace, in 1736, of James Watt, who was born in a house on Dalrymple Street.

◀ **Barrhead**
Graham Street c1918 B270004
By this time, calico-printing was losing its position as the town's main industry, and the production of porcelain sanitary ware was taking over.

▼ **Greenock**
The Harbour 1904 52632
During the late 17th century, Greenock's herring trade with France and the Baltic required a fleet of more than 300 boats. The town motto was 'Let herring swim that trade maintain'. The herring went elsewhere, and the trade declined.

◀ **Greenock**
Princes Pier 1904 52634
An excursion steamer manoeuvres alongside Princes Pier. Owned by the Glasgow & South Western Railway, the pier was rebuilt and extended during 1892-94 and more than £20,000 was spent by the company on alterations to the pier railway station. The new buildings featured four Italianate towers constructed of red Ruabon brick.

Greenock
The View from
Whinhill 1899 43400
It was in the 17th century that Greenock developed as a port, providing a packet service to and from Ireland. During the early years of the 18th century, facilities were improved with the construction of a harbour and quays. By 1760, the first shipyards at Greenock were open, and in 1786 a graving dock was completed. A new graving dock was built in the early 1870s and work on the James Watt Dock began in 1881. In this view, we see the smoking chimneypots of Greenock and the entrance to Gare Loch.

Gourock, From Tower Hill 1900 45965
Gourock was among the towns where witch hunts took place during the 17th century. One of the unfortunates who was burnt at the stake was Mary Lamont. The girl confessed, probably under torture, that she intended to throw Granny Kempock's Stone, a pre-historic monolith standing 6 ft high, into the sea so that ships might be wrecked upon it. In this view, the steamer crossing West Bay is turning to berth at the pier.

Gourock, From the Pier 1900 45975
This view shows the backs of buildings along Kempock Street. Kempock Place is just in view on the extreme left. Over to the right is Seaton's temperance hotel, one of several in the town. At this time, temperance hotels abounded throughout the UK, but there was in fact little difference between them and private hotels because neither had liquor licences.

Gourock, Kempock Street 1900 45978
The total absence of road traffic, other than bicycles, and the fact that people appear to be in their best clothes, suggests that this picture was taken on a Sunday. Note the blinds on the shop windows and the attraction they hold for small boys.

Gourock, The Esplanade 1900 45969
As well as being a resort, Gourock was known for its herring curing. In 1688, the first recorded curing of red herrings took place here. Here we can see the pebble beach.

▼ Clydebank, Glasgow Road 1900 C208004

Situated on the Clyde, opposite the mouth of the River Cart, Clydebank was little more than farmland until 1871-72, when J & G Thomson began the construction of a shipyard. Clydebank went into production in 1872 with three steamers for Thomas Skinner of Glasgow. A town eventually grew up on land behind the shipyard. On the left is the Clydebank Co-operative, a teetotal organisation which banned its members from selling alcohol until 1959.

▼ Clydebank, Glasgow Road 1900 C208005

Everyone in this picture seems to be watching the cameraman. Electric trams first ran in Glasgow in 1898 on the Mitchell Street to Springburn route. By 1909, there were about 95 miles of double-track tramway, including lines to Govan, Partick, Pollockshaws and Rutherglen.

▲ Clydebank Kilbowie Road 1900
C208002

In 1881, the population of Clydebank was 1,600 people, most of whom depended upon the shipyard. In 1882, the American firm of Singers opened a sewing-machine factory, bringing yet more jobs and more people to the area. Clydebank became a burgh in 1886. The swelling population certainly seems to be causing congestion on this narrow bridge.

◄ **Dumbarton
The Castle 1897** 39809
It was from here, in 1548,
that six-year-old Mary,
Queen of Scots left for
France to marry the
Dauphin when both were
old enough. In return,
France offered Scotland
military assistance against
England.

36

Helensburgh
The Esplanade 1901
47402
The coming of the railways put Helensburgh into the Glasgow commuter belt, whilst its steamer connections helped it to develop as a holiday centre. In the distance and slightly to the left of the clock tower is the obelisk erected to the memory of Henry Bell, who built the first steam-powered vessel to sail on the Clyde. Another famous son of the town was J Logie Baird, the inventor of television.

Helensburgh, Colquhoun Square 1901 47405
Sir James Colquhoun of Luss developed Helensburgh in the late 18th century as a residential district for those who could afford not to have to live any nearer to Glasgow than was absolutely necessary. Helensburgh's leading hotels were the Queen's and the Imperial. During the main season, rooms cost from 3s 6d a day and dinner was 4s, which was slightly less than what the top Glasgow hotels were charging.

Helensburgh, Princes Street 1901 47404
Helensburgh was described as 'a favourite watering place situated at the mouth of the Gareloch, laid out with the mathematical regularity of an American city'.

39

Loch Lomond, The Pier at Tarbet 1899 43209
Loch Lomond became a popular destination for day trippers from around Clydeside, especially after the opening of the Dumbarton & Balloch Joint Railway. The loch itself was served by the steamers of the Loch Lomond Steam Boat Company, whose first ship, the 'Prince of Wales', was built at Port Glasgow in 1858. Tarbet lies at the eastern end of a narrow neck of land that extends from Arrochar on Loch Long.

40

Dunoon, The Pier 1904 52620
Until the early 19th century, Dunoon was nothing more than a small village clustered around a castle. The popularity of the Clyde excursion steamers changed all that: Dunoon developed into a holiday resort, the largest and best known on the Cowal. One steamer has just departed and there are two others alongside. The one on the right appears to belong to the North British Railway'. Dunoon handled 10,000 calls by steamers every year.

Dunoon
The Argyll Hotel 1904
52614
This was one of three hotels recommended to overseas visitors; the others were the Queen's and McColl's. It was also possible to hire apartments in Dunoon at about 15s a week during the main season.

▼ **Rothesay, The Glenburn Hydropathic 1899** 43210
A week's stay here cost around 59s. Although guests were not obliged to·take any of the water treatments offered, they were expected to refrain from drinking alcohol and had to take their meals together at prescribed hours.

▼ **Rothesay, The Esplanade 1897** 39838
A horse-tram from Port Bannatyne makes its way along Rothesay Esplanade. The tramway extended to Ettrick Bay on the west coast and was electrified in 1902.

▲ **Rothesay
The Esplanade 1897**
39837
Rothesay's main hotels at this time were the Royal, the Queen's, and the Bute Arms. The Esplanade Hotel offered tea, bed and breakfast for 8s 6d per night.

44

◀ **Rothesay**
The Castle 1897 39845
An earlier castle on this site
was captured in 1263 by
the Norse and was subse-
quently demolished,
allegedly on the orders of
Robert the Bruce. A new,
stronger fortress was then
built in its place. Here we
see a bridge across the
moat.

Rothesay
The Pier 1897 39836
The first effective
spinning mill in the west
of Scotland was built at
Rothesay. Between
1787 and 1834, the
number of cotton mills
in Scotland rocketed
from just 19 to 134.
During the American
Civil War American
imports of cotton fell
from 8,600 tons in
1861 to 350 tons in
1864. This in turn
caused severe distress
and hardship amongst
British mill workers.
During the season,
Rothesay's population
of about 9,000 would
increase dramatically.

**Arran
The Castle and Loch
Ranza c1890** A93001
This view was
photographed near the
northern tip of the island.
A ruined 14th-century
double-towered castle
stands guard over Loch
Ranza. It was here that
Robert Bruce is said to
have landed on his return
from Ireland in 1306.

Tarbert, At the Head of East Loch Tarbert 1890 T102001
This is an inlet of Loch Fyne. West Loch Tarbert is only a couple of miles away; it is said that in 1093 Magnus Barefoot dragged his longship overland between the two lochs, claiming Kintyre as a Norse possession.

Millport, General View 1897 39857
The Collegiate Church built in 1851 was consecrated as the Episcopal Cathedral of Argyll and the Isles in 1876. Famous for the quality of its beaches, Millport developed as a resort following the construction of the harbour and the introduction of a ferry service to and from Largs. As late as the 1940s, there was only one bus, a few motor taxis and some horse-drawn cabs on the island.

Largs, General View 1897 39851

The bustling holiday town of Largs has long been famous as the site of a battle in 1263 between the Norwegians and the Scots. The Battle of Largs was important because it led to the Treaty of Perth, under which Man and the Western Isles were purchased by the Scottish crown. Sheltered by the nearby island of Cumbrae, Largs has long been a popular place for messing about in boats. It was also a good centre for excursions by steamer.

Largs, The Church of St Columba 1897 39855

This 17th-century church is famous for the Skelmorlie Aisle, which contains the tombs of Sir Robert Montgomery and his wife. Another famous monument, the round tower at Bowen Craig, commemorated the defeat of the Norsemen in 1263.

52

53

◄ **Irvine**
Eglinton Castle 1904
53151
Standing between
Kilwinning and Irvine,
the castle became
famous in 1839 as the
venue for a medieval
tournament. Though not
the first tournament to
be held in Europe during
the 19th century, it was
the first and last to be
held in the UK during
the Gothic revival. In full
armour, knights rode
down the lists, trying to
unhorse one another
with lances.

◀ **Largs**
The Church and the
Seafront 1897 39856
Largs was well-served by
steamers from all parts of the
Clyde, and by the Glasgow &
South Western Railway to
Ardrossan via Fairlie and
West Kilbride. One of Largs's
own well-travelled sons was
Sir Thomas Brisbane, who
became governor of New
South Wales and had an
Australian city named after
him.

▼ **Irvine**
The Harbour 1904 53154
A royal burgh and port, Irvine was,
by the 1920s, a town of 7,000
inhabitants. Many of these were
employed in ironworking, chemical
manufacturing and coal-mining, or
in Nobel's dynamite works at
Ardeer.The novelist John Galt was
born in the town in 1779, but
Irvine is more famous as the place
where Robert Burns eked out a
living as a flax-dresser between
1781 and 1783.

54

◀ **Ayr**
Twa Brigs 1900 46000
The 'Twa Brigs of Ayr'
became famous thanks
to a poem by Robert
Burns. Things had
changed by the time this
photograph was taken.
The Auld Brig, which is
thought to date from the
13th century, is still
standing. The New Brig
was rebuilt in 1879
having lasted less than
100 years.

55

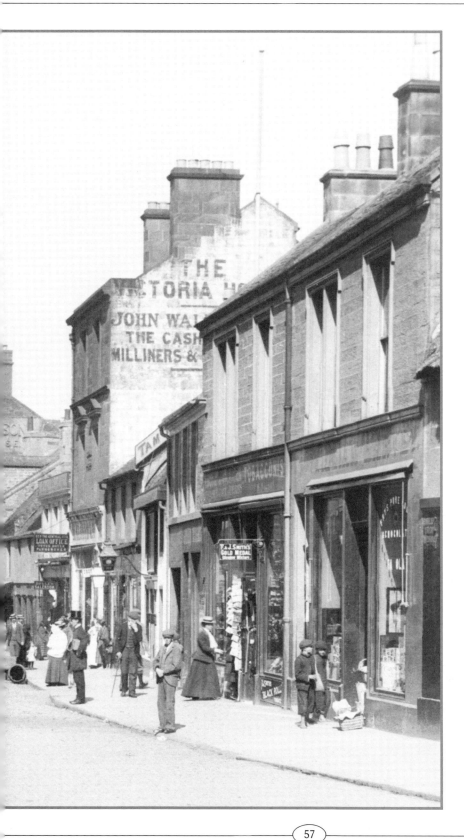

56

Ayr
The Wallace Tower
and High Street 1900
46002
Little survives of the old
town, although parts the
former Greyfriars
church of St John,
where Robert the Bruce
held a Parliament in
1315, are thought to
date back to its
beginnings.The 130 ft
high neo-Gothic
Wallace Tower, situated
in the High Street, was
completed in 1832.
It replaced an earlier
structure in which
Sir William Wallace was
alleged to have been
imprisoned.

Ayr, Sandgate Street 1900 46003
Famous as the birthplace of John Macadam in 1756 and of Robert Burns in 1759, Ayr was founded under a charter granted by William the Lion. This view looks towards the New Brig and Main Street. On the right, at the junction with the High Street, are the town buildings, the handsome spire of which is considered to be one of the finest in the Lowlands.

Alloway, The Birthplace of Robert Burns 1897 39858
Robert Burns was born here on 25 January 1759. The cottage was rebuilt by the poet's father and later became an inn. In 1881 it was purchased by the trustees of the Burns Monument and opened as a museum.

Alloway, The Kirk 1897 39861
This roofless church is alleged to be haunted. Burns's father is buried in the churchyard.

The Highlands and Islands

Glencoe 1890 G81001
At dawn on 13 February 1692, soldiers commanded by Campbell of Glen Lyon killed at least 40 out of the 200 MacDonalds living in this glen. Among the dead was the MacDonald chieftain MacIan of Glencoe, who was buried on the island of Eilean Munde.

▼ **Glencoe 1890** 43199

The reason for the Glencoe massacre was the failure of MacIan to swear allegiance to William III before 1 January 1692. MacIan had arrived at Fort William on 31 December, but was redirected to Inveraray, with the result that he did not take the oath until 6 January.

▼ **Inverlochy, The Castle c1890** 130001

It was here in February 1645, after a forced march across difficult terrain in appalling weather, that the Marquis of Montrose with 1,500 troops defeated a 5,000 strong force of Campbells and Lowlanders. The clan power of Argyll is said to have been destroyed for a generation.

▲ **Isle of Skye Kyleakin c1890** K53001
At Kyleakin stand the ruins of Castle Moil. It is said that the castle was built by the daughter of one of the Norse kings of the Western Isles. Legend has it that she had a boom placed across the strait, and any ship plying between Skye and the mainland had to pay a toll. The town overlooks the narrow strait of Kyle Akin, which is said to take its name from King Haakon who sailed this way in 1263.

**◄ Glenfinnan
Loch Shiel c1890** L135001
Prince Charles Edward
Stuart landed at Glenfinnan
on 19 August 1745. Here,
with a few loyal retainers,
Prince Charles waited for
the clans. After three hours
only 150 men of the clan
Ranald had joined him.
Then Cameron of Lochiel
arrived with about 700
clansmen, followed by the
MacDonalds of Keppoch.
The royal standard was
raised, and the fight to
regain the throne for the
house of Stuart was on.

Glen Torridon 1890 G80001
This wild and rocky landscape is typical of the Highlands. The quartzite peaks of Beinn Eighe are in the background. The UK's first National Nature Reserve was some miles away on the slopes of Sgurr Ban.

Isle of Mull, Duart Castle 1903 M114001
This is the ancestral home of the chiefs of the Macleans. The Macleans paid the price for siding with James VII against William III, forfeiting castle and estates. Duart was then garrisoned until the end of the 18th century, when it was allowed to fall into ruin. Purchased back by Sir Fitzroy Maclean, Duart has been completely restored.

Corpach, Loch Eil 1890 B267001
In the background to the south-east is Ben Nevis. The mountain once boasted a hostel and an observatory on its summit. The observatory lasted from 1883 to 1904, and the hostel closed in 1915.

Staffa, Fingal's Cave 1903 50897
Lying to the north-east of Iona, the uninhabited island of Staffa is famous for its caves and rock formations. Legend has it that the cave was formed when the giant Finn McCoul made the island. Finn is also said to have built the giant's causeway in Northern Ireland.

**Iona
Cottages by the Shore
1903** 50887
Iona lies just off the
extreme south-west of
Mull. In 1203, the
Benedictines founded a
monastery on the island
which lasted until the
Reformation. In 1899,
the 8th Duke of Argyll
presented the ruins of the
abbey to the Church of
Scotland in the hope that
restoration work might be
undertaken. The building
was eventually re-roofed,
and used for worship
once again in 1910.

**Iona
The Cathedral 1903**
50889

It was chosen by St Columba in AD 563 as the site for a religious house from where he could carry out his missionary work. St Columba was a member of the O'Neill clan; he left Ireland after the battle of Cuil-dremne. It is said that it was Columba himself who caused the battle: he was accused by the High King of taking a psalter without permission, so Columba appealed to his clan for help in clearing his name, and the matter was settled by sword and axe.

◄ **Oban**
The Dog Stone or
Clach a Choin 1901
47513
The legendary Fingal is said to have tied his dog Bran to the stone. In the distance is the ruined McDougall fortress of Dunollie Castle, which overlooks the Firth of Lorne.

◀ Iona
St Oran's Chapel 1903
50892
The ruined Romanesque chapel stands by the grave-yard. Iona is the oldest Christian burial ground in Scotland and contains the graves of many kings and chieftains. Among those buried here are Kenneth MacAlpine, the first Celtic king of Scotland, and Duncan, who was murdered by Macbeth in 1040.

▼ Oban
George Street 1901 47511
Fishing and agriculture played an important part in the economy of the area, but it was the opening up of the Western Highlands to tourism that gave the town the boost it so desperately needed. On the right is the Caledonian Hotel, one of a number of hotels in the town. The Great Western and the Alexandria were the most expensive, and the Marine was well spoken of. There were three temperance hotels, one of which can be seen next to the King's Arms.

◀ Oban
The Sound of Kerrera 1903 50885
The Island of Kerrera faces Oban and is linked to the town by a ferry service. On the island is the ruined Gylen Castle, where king Alexander II died of fever in 1249. There is also a memorial to David Hutcheson, the pioneer of steamboat services to the Western Isles.

70

Oban
The Bay c1900 04001
The town of Oban is only a little more than 200 years old. It owes its origins to the establishing of a fishing station by the government Fishery Board in 1786. The aim had been to develop commercial fishing in the Firth of Lorne. The project was eventually abandoned, but by this time Oban had begun to develop, albeit very slowly. The railway station is in the foreground with the north pier and esplanade on the far side of the bay beyond the yachts and steamers.

Inverary, By the Loch c1915 115003
Time for a paddle - two well-dressed ladies rather daringly show their legs.

Inverary, General View 1899 43200
Inverary Castle, the 18th-century home of the Dukes of Argyll, was designed by Roger Morris and Robert Mylne and completed in about 1780. During his visit to the Highlands, Dr Johnson was entertained here by the 5th Duke. The town was originally closer to the old castle, but was relocated in the mid 18th century. It was to Inverary that MacIan of Glencoe was sent to swear allegiance to William III. MacIan's unavoidable delay in reaching Inverary led to the massacre of Glencoe.

Fortrose, Street Scene 1880 F60002
Fortrose stands on the Black Isle overlooking the inner Moray Firth. The ruined cathedral dates from the reign of David I. Some of the stone was taken by Cromwell's forces for use in the construction of a fort at Inverness. Fortrose was originally called Chanonry. It was made a royal burgh in 1592. In January of that year a hoard of silver coins dating from the time of Robert III were unearthed near the ruins of the cathedral.

73

74

◄ **Dingwall**
General View 1890 D77001
Dingwall stands on the Cromarty Firth. It was the home town of General Hector MacDonald (1853-1903), who enlisted in the 92nd Highlanders at the age of 17. In 1879, MacDonald distinguished himself during the First Afghan War, and General Roberts offered him a Victoria Cross or a commission. He chose the commission, saying that he would win the Victoria Cross later.

◄ Strathpeffer
Washing Day c1890
S421003

This village was a popular spa, having both sulphur and chalybeate springs. It was served by a branch line of the Highland Railway from Fodderty Junction. Are these girls laundresses at one of the hotels?

▼ Inverness
The View from Inverness Castle c1890
I255003

The area in and around Inverness has been occupied since ancient times and it was here, in the 6th century, that the capital of the Pictish kingdom stood. It is thought that Macbeth may have lived at Inverness Castle, or used it as a base for operations against the Orcadians. The suspension bridge superseded a stone bridge of seven arches which was destroyed during severe flooding in 1849. The suspension bridge itself lasted until 1961, when it was demolished.

◄ Culloden Moor
The Battlefield c1890
I255001

In 1746 Prince Charles Edward Stuart fought at the battle of Culloden Moor. Following the battle, 300 clansmen were herded into Inverness town jail and left without food or water for two days. Those that died were thrown into unmarked trenches. On the right is the memorial cairn built in 1881 by Arthur Forbes of Culloden.

Cawdor
The Castle c1890
C212001
A few miles to the south of Nairn stands Cawdor Castle, one of Scotland's finest medieval buildings. It is famous for its association with Macbeth and the murder of Duncan. The keep dates from 1454, and some parts are thought to be even older. The castle was extensively altered during the 16th and 17th centuries and again in the 19th.

Grampian

Braemar, The Mill on the Cluny 1880 B266002
The village of Braemar is situated on the banks of
Cluny Burn. It was here, in 1715, that a number of
Scottish lords, including the Earl of Mar, met on
the pretext of a hunting trip to plan an uprising
against the House of Hanover and return the
Stuarts to the throne of Scotland. Among later
visitors to the village was Robert Louis Stevenson:
while spending a winter here he wrote 'Treasure
Island'.

▼ Braemar, The Cairnwell Pass 1879 B266003
The road south from Braemar climbs through Glen Clunie and then
over the rugged Cairnwell Pass.

▼ Aberdeen, The Auld Brig O' Bargowure 1890 A90304
Aberdeen is now Scotland's third largest city. Its charters date back to
c1179, although St Machar is said to have founded a church here in AD
580. This single-span bridge is situated a few hundred yards to the
north of St Machar's Cathedral. It dates from the early 14th century.

**▲ Fraserburgh
The Herring Fleet
c1900** F63002
Fraserburgh was founded
in the 16th century in a
charter granted to the
7th Laird of Philorth. In
1595, a university was
founded, but it lasted
only a decade or so - its
principal was arrested on
the orders of James VI.
The university never
recovered and faded into
obscurity. Fishing was an
important local industry:
in 1914 there were more
than 200 boats registered
here.

◄ **Aberdeen**
Union Street c1885 A90305
These days, Aberdeen is
famous for its association with
North Sea oil, but shipbuilding,
fishing, papermaking and the
quarrying of granite have all
played their part in the city's
development. On the right of
this view is the Mercat Cross,
which dates from 1686. It was
built at a cost of £100, paid for
out of guild wine funds.
Beyond the cross are the
municipal buildings complete
with their 210 ft tower.

**Aberdeen
Union Street c1899**
A90309
Electric tramcars compete
with a horse and cart in
this crowded street.
The chief thoroughfare of
Aberdeen, Union Street
at this time was three-
quarters of a mile long,
70 ft wide and built
entirely of granite.

Aberdeen, Queen's Corner and St Nicholas Street c1899 A90307
Here we see another tramcar and more granite setts. There is some activity around the base of the statue - are the two ladies selling flowers and button-holes?

Aberdeen, Union Terrace and Gardens c1899 A90308
Nearby is the Grand Hotel (rooms 4s 6d, dinner 5s), the parish council building, the school board offices and a statue of Robert Burns.

Dunnottar Castle c1900 D80401
The castle stands to the south of Stonehaven on a rocky headland overlooking the North Sea. It was here, in July 1650, that Charles II was entertained by the Earl Marischal. It was the only fortress in Scotland that flew the Stuart royal flag after Charles's defeat at Worcester in 1651. Dunnottar held out until May 1652, when Sir George Ogilvy of Barras was allowed to surrender with all the honours of war.

Tayside

Brechin, David Street 1900 B275002
This small town once played host to one of the sig-
nificant events in Scotland's history: John Balliol
surrendered the realm of Scotland to Edward
Longshanks here on 10 July 1296. When Balliol
walked into Brechin Castle to meet Bishop Anthony
Bek of Durham, the Bishop ripped the red and gold
arms of Scotland off Balliol's tunic. Balliol was
known afterwards as Toom(empty) Tabard.
Brechin's famous landmark was the Round Tower,
dating from the 10th or 11th century and one of
only two examples of round towers in Scotland.

◀ **Pert
h High Street East 1899**
43899
By this time the population
of Perth was about 32,000.
The city's manufacturing
industries were diverse and
included linen, twine, jute,
glassmaking and printing.

Perth
Moncrieffe Island and the Tay 1901 47430
Cutting across the middle of the picture is the bridge carrying the Caledonian Railway, while on the far right is the Victoria Road bridge. Between the two are the county buildings, which occupy the site of the house in which the Gowrie conspiracy against James VI was hatched in 1600.

Perth
The Post Office and New Scott Street 1899 43901
An ancient royal burgh, Perth was once capital of Scotland. It was at Perth, in 1559, that John Knox gave his famous sermon from the pulpit of St John's Church, a powerful and emotive speech against idolatry which is regarded by many as the start of the Reformation in Scotland. Among documents preserved locally is a letter written by John Blair dated 7 November 1689. Blair was the postmaster-general, and in the letter he details the establishment of a postal service in the city.

Perth
The Bridge 1899 43897
Built of rose-red sandstone, Perth Bridge was completed in 1771. The city then had a population of nearly 8,000. It was still an important port, with several hundred vessels coming up river every year to discharge and take on cargo.

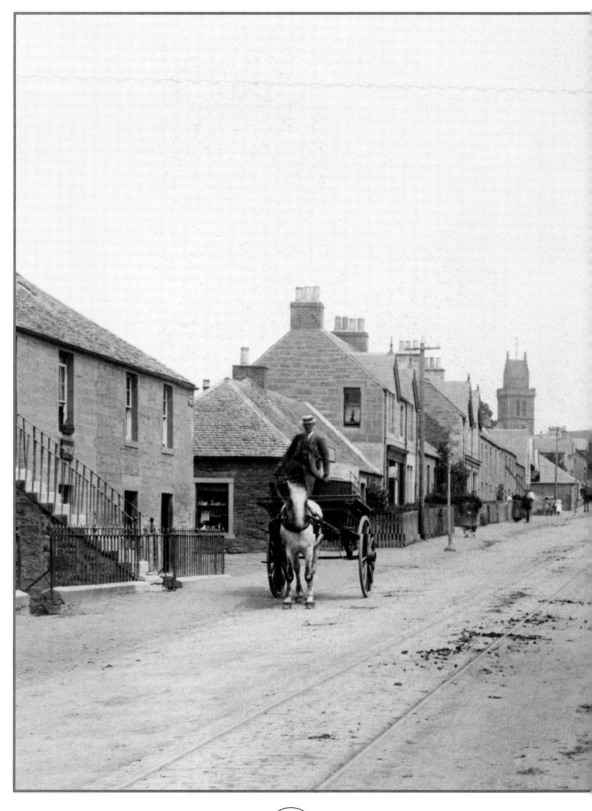

90

Scone
The Village 1899
43917
Scone was where
Scotland's kings were
crowned. On 1 January
1651, Charles II was
crowned king of
Scotland with Robert
the Bruce's gold circlet.
His coronation was
bought at a price.
Charles agreed to
impose the Presbyterian
Church in England, and
the third civil war was
about to begin.

Crieff, Comrie Street 1904 52682
Crieff was originally called Drummond. In January 1716, the place was totally destroyed when the Jacobites put the town to the torch. It was rebuilt thanks to the efforts of James Drummond, 3rd Duke of Perth.

Crieff, High Street 1899 43926
On his retreat north in 1745, Prince Charles Edward Stuart held a council of war in Crieff at the Drummond Arms.

93

Comrie, View from the East 1899 44405
Situated between Crieff and St Fillans on the Highland fault line, Comrie is famous for the number of earth tremors experienced by its inhabitants. The first recorded tremor was in 1789, and the most sustained were a series of 20 within 24 hours in 1839.

Central Scotland and Fife

Killin, The Mill 1890 K51004
The mill stands on the River Dochart. Not far away
is the ruined Breadalbane stronghold of Finlarig
Castle. One of its more interesting features is what
is thought to be an ancient beheading pit.

▼ **Loch Katrine c1890** L93002
An excursion steamer waits at the pier. The loch, which is ringed with hills, features in Sir Walter Scott's poem 'The Lady of the Lake'.

▼ **Loch Achray c1899** 44603
This small loch is sandwiched between Loch Katrine and Loch Vennachar. This picture shows the Trossachs Hotel situated on the northern shore, and the wooded slopes of Sron Armailte.

▲ **Dunblane
The Bridge and the
Cathedral 1899** 44651
The body of the cathedral dates from the 13th century; the tower is Norman. During the 16th century, the roof of the nave collapsed and was not finally restored until 1893.

96

97

**Bridge of Allan
Street Scene 1899** 44675
Robert Louis Stevenson was
a frequent visitor to Bridge
of Allan when the town was
a popular Victorian spa
complete with pump room
and baths.

◄ **Stirling**
Old Parliament House
1899 44697
It was here that both James II and James V were born and where Mary, Queen of Scots and James VI both lived for a number of years. The Parliament Hall is close to the Inner Court and James VI's Chapel Royal. Following their defeat at the Battle of Dunbar, Major General David Leslie and several thousand survivors of his army took shelter in Stirling. The town eventually fell to General Monk.

◄ **Stirling**
Broad Street 1899 44705
This view looks towards Mar's Wark: dating from 1570, this uncompleted renaissance building was intended for use by the Earl of Mar who was Regent.

▼ **Stirling**
The Castle 1899 44696
One of Scotland's greatest royal fortresses, Stirling Castle was taken by William Wallace in 1297 but was surrendered to Edward I in August 1305 following a siege.
The survivors of the garrison, commanded by Sir William Oliphant, were brought before Longshanks and made to kneel in supplication.

◄ **Stirling**
The Bridge 1899 44701
Stirling is the last place where there is a bridge over the Forth before the river widens into an estuary. The town and its castle have therefore been fought over on numerous occasions. Dating from about 1400, the bridge was for years one of only a handful of crossing points over the Forth. In 1745, one of the arches was blown up to prevent Prince Charles Edward's forces from entering the town.

102

**Aberdour
The Pier 1900** 45912
Aberdour in the
Kingdom of Fife, lying
between Burntisland
and Dalgety Bay, is
described in the 1906
Baedeker as 'a favourite
little sea-bathing place,
with an old castle and
the ruins of a Norman
church'. In this view, an
excursion steamer from
Leith lies at the end of
the curving stone pier.

Lothian

Edinburgh

The Old Town, as it was called, grew eastward along the ridge from the castle down to where Holyroodhouse would eventually be built. Much of the Old Town was rebuilt in the middle of the 16th century following a major fire, but even then it remained notoriously cramped and insanitary. The only way for the inhabitants to get rid of their refuse and empty their chamber pots was by throwing their rubbish into the street at night. There were refuse men who came in the wee small hours to shovel it up and cart it away; but on Dr Johnson's first visit to Edinburgh in August 1773, he is said to have met Boswell in the High Street with the words 'Sir, I smell you in the dark'.

The New Town dates from 1768 and is centred on the three parallel thoroughfares of Princes Street, George Street and Charlotte Street.

103

Linlithgow, Street Scene 1897 39157
All is peace and quiet in this scene, but things were livelier on 23 January 1570. Lord James Stewart, Earl of Moray and Regent, was shot by James Hamilton as he rode through the town. The assassin fired his musket from an upper window in a house belonging to the archbishop of St Andrews, who also appears to have supplied the getaway horse. The archbishop was executed at Stirling in 1571 without the formality of a trial.

Linlithgow Palace 1897 39154
The Palace is situated upon the south shore of Linlithgow Loch. It was here in 1542 that Mary, Queen of Scots was born in 1542. The palace is thought to have been burnt down accidently in 1746 by General Hawley's troops.

Edinburgh, Holyrood House 1897 39168
Work on the palace began during the reign of James IV and continued under James V. On the left are the remains of the Chapel Royal, which is in fact the nave of an abbey founded in 1128.

Edinburgh, The Canongate Tolbooth 1897 39124A
Note the poles used for drying washing. When this picture was taken, the tolbooth was already more than 300 years old, having been built at the end of the 16th century. It has had a varied career, having been used as a courthouse and a prison.

106

Edinburgh, The Castle from Johnston Terrace 1897 39120
Though he managed to occupy the city in 1745, Prince Charles Edward Stuart failed to capture its fortress.

107

**Edinburgh
The Grassmarket
1883** E24303
This was the site of many an execution and the location of the Porteous Riots in 1736. John Porteous was appointed captain of one of the companies employed to keep the peace. At a riot following the execution of a man named Robertson, Porteous ordered his men to fire on the crowd. He was later taken into custody, tried and condemned to death, but a stay of execution was granted. On 7 September, a mob broke into the jail and lynched him in the Grassmarket.

▼ **Edinburgh, The Scott Monument c1900** E24510
The monument was designed by George Kemp and completed in
1844. During his lifetime Scott lived at several addresses in the city,
the most famous being 39 Castle Street, where he wrote many of the
Waverley novels.

▼ **Edinburgh, Prince's Street, West End 1897** 39113
This was the fashionable place to shop and eat out; there were several
highly recommended restaurants, including Ferguson & Forrester,
Littlejohns and the Royal British. Leading confectioners were Mackies
and Ritchies, where shortbread was a speciality.

▲ **Edinburgh
Prince's Street 1897**
39108
This view looks west
along the main thorough-
fare of the New Town,
with Prince's Street
Gardens on the left.

**Edinburgh
Waverley Bridge 1883**
E24302
Cockburn Street twists and
climbs up to the High
Street. On the right, the
famous crown spire of
St Giles's Church can be
seen above the rooftops.

**Edinburgh
The Castle from Prince's
Gardens 1897** 39119
The gardens and the
railway occupy what was
the Nor' Loch, an expanse
of water that formed part of
the old city's defences. It
was drained at the same
time as nearby marshland
in the late 18th century to
allow Edinburgh to grow.

◄ Edinburgh
Hope Street 1887 39114
Here we see the junction of
Hope Street, Queensferry
Street and Sandwick Street.
St John's and St Cuthbert's
churches provide the backdrop
along with the castle .

▼ Newhaven
The Harbour 1897 39139
A little more than one mile
to the west of Leith is the
small fishing village of
Newhaven. It was here that
James IV founded a royal
dockyard where he could
build his navy. The first ship
that was launched was the
'Great Michael', a huge
warship capable of carrying
420 gunners and 1,000
soldiers.

◄ Newhaven
Fishermen's Cottages
1897 39137
The fishermen's wives
were noted for their
dresses, which probably
reflected their Dutch and
Scandinavian origins.
They were also known
for their cries when
selling fish: 'Caller
Herrin' (fresh herrings)
and 'Caller Ou' (fresh
oysters).

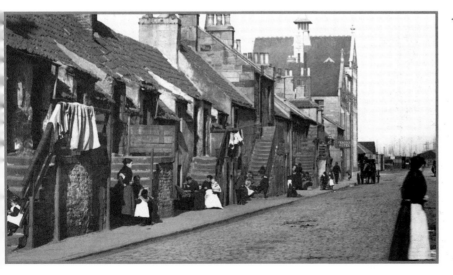

117

The Forth Bridge 1897
39145
Built between 1883 and 1890, the bridge was constructed to carry the North British Railway's main line between Edinburgh and Aberdeen. It has an overall length of 2,700 yards including approach viaducts.
The tracks run across the bridge 150 ft above sea level.

118

**North Berwick
Quality Street 1897**
39176
The opening of the railway branch line put North Berwick within easy reach of Edinburgh, making it a popular place for people working in Edinburgh to live; it was also a popular place for holidays and outings.

North Berwick, The Marine Hotel and the Golf Links 1897 39177
By the beginning of the 20th century, North Berwick was beginning to rival St Andrews. Prices for rooms and meals at the Marine and the Royal hotels were on a par with the top hotels in central Glasgow and Edinburgh.

Tantallon Castle 1897 39186
This mighty fortress, with its distinctive rose-red brickwork, was a Douglas stronghold. It was destroyed by General Monk's troops in 1651. The small island in the background is the Bass Rock.

Index

Frith Book Co Titles

www.francisfrith.co.uk

The Frith Book Company publishes over 100 new titles each year. A selection of those currently available is listed below. For latest catalogue please contact Frith Book Co.
Town Books 96 pages, approximately 100 photos. **County and Themed Books** 128 pages, approximately 150 photos (unless specified). All titles hardback with laminated case and jacket except those indicated pb (paperback)

Amersham, Chesham & Rickmansworth (pb)	1-85937-340-2	£9.99	Devon (pb)	1-85937-297-x	£9.99
Andover (pb)	1-85937-292-9	£9.99	Devon Churches (pb)	1-85937-250-3	£9.99
Aylesbury (pb)	1-85937-227-9	£9.99	Dorchester (pb)	1-85937-307-0	£9.99
Barnstaple (pb)	1-85937-300-3	£9.99	Dorset (pb)	1-85937-269-4	£9.99
Basildon Living Memories (pb)	1-85937-515-4	£9.99	Dorset Coast (pb)	1-85937-299-6	£9.99
Bath (pb)	1-85937-419-0	£9.99	Dorset Living Memories (pb)	1-85937-584-7	£9.99
Bedford (pb)	1-85937-205-8	£9.99	Down the Severn (pb)	1-85937-560-x	£9.99
Bedfordshire Living Memories	1-85937-513-8	£14.99	Down The Thames (pb)	1-85937-278-3	£9.99
Belfast (pb)	1-85937-303-8	£9.99	Down the Trent	1-85937-311-9	£14.99
Berkshire (pb)	1-85937-191-4	£9.99	East Anglia (pb)	1-85937-265-1	£9.99
Berkshire Churches	1-85937-170-1	£17.99	East Grinstead (pb)	1-85937-138-8	£9.99
Berkshire Living Memories	1-85937-332-1	£14.99	East London	1-85937-080-2	£14.99
Black Country	1-85937-497-2	£12.99	East Sussex (pb)	1-85937-606-1	£9.99
Blackpool (pb)	1-85937-393-3	£9.99	Eastbourne (pb)	1-85937-399-2	£9.99
Bognor Regis (pb)	1-85937-431-x	£9.99	Edinburgh (pb)	1-85937-193-0	£8.99
Bournemouth (pb)	1-85937-545-6	£9.99	England In The 1880s	1-85937-331-3	£17.99
Bradford (pb)	1-85937-204-x	£9.99	Essex - Second Selection	1-85937-456-5	£14.99
Bridgend (pb)	1-85937-386-0	£7.99	Essex (pb)	1-85937-270-8	£9.99
Bridgwater (pb)	1-85937-305-4	£9.99	Essex Coast	1-85937-342-9	£14.99
Bridport (pb)	1-85937-327-5	£9.99	Essex Living Memories	1-85937-490-5	£14.99
Brighton (pb)	1-85937-192-2	£8.99	Exeter	1-85937-539-1	£9.99
Bristol (pb)	1-85937-264-3	£9.99	Exmoor (pb)	1-85937-608-8	£9.99
British Life A Century Ago (pb)	1-85937-213-9	£9.99	Falmouth (pb)	1-85937-594-4	£9.99
Buckinghamshire (pb)	1-85937-200-7	£9.99	Folkestone (pb)	1-85937-124-8	£9.99
Camberley (pb)	1-85937-222-8	£9.99	Frome (pb)	1-85937-317-8	£9.99
Cambridge (pb)	1-85937-422-0	£9.99	Glamorgan	1-85937-488-3	£14.99
Cambridgeshire (pb)	1-85937-420-4	£9.99	Glasgow (pb)	1-85937-190-6	£9.99
Cambridgeshire Villages	1-85937-523-5	£14.99	Glastonbury (pb)	1-85937-338-0	£7.99
Canals And Waterways (pb)	1-85937-291-0	£9.99	Gloucester (pb)	1-85937-232-5	£9.99
Canterbury Cathedral (pb)	1-85937-179-5	£9.99	Gloucestershire (pb)	1-85937-561-8	£9.99
Cardiff (pb)	1-85937-093-4	£9.99	Great Yarmouth (pb)	1-85937-426-3	£9.99
Carmarthenshire (pb)	1-85937-604-5	£9.99	Greater Manchester (pb)	1-85937-266-x	£9.99
Chelmsford (pb)	1-85937-310-0	£9.99	Guildford (pb)	1-85937-410-7	£9.99
Cheltenham (pb)	1-85937-095-0	£9.99	Hampshire (pb)	1-85937-279-1	£9.99
Cheshire (pb)	1-85937-271-6	£9.99	Harrogate (pb)	1-85937-423-9	£9.99
Chester (pb)	1-85937-382 8	£9.99	Hastings and Bexhill (pb)	1-85937-131-0	£9.99
Chesterfield (pb)	1-85937-378-x	£9.99	Heart of Lancashire (pb)	1-85937-197-3	£9.99
Chichester (pb)	1-85937-228-7	£9.99	Helston (pb)	1-85937-214-7	£9.99
Churches of East Cornwall (pb)	1-85937-249-x	£9.99	Hereford (pb)	1-85937-175-2	£9.99
Churches of Hampshire (pb)	1-85937-207-4	£9.99	Herefordshire (pb)	1-85937-567-7	£9.99
Cinque Ports & Two Ancient Towns	1-85937-492-1	£14.99	Herefordshire Living Memories	1-85937-514-6	£14.99
Colchester (pb)	1-85937-188-4	£8.99	Hertfordshire (pb)	1-85937-247-3	£9.99
Cornwall (pb)	1-85937-229-5	£9.99	Horsham (pb)	1-85937-432-8	£9.99
Cornwall Living Memories	1-85937-248-1	£14.99	Humberside (pb)	1-85937-605-3	£9.99
Cotswolds (pb)	1-85937-230-9	£9.99	Hythe, Romney Marsh, Ashford (pb)	1-85937-256-2	£9.99
Cotswolds Living Memories	1-85937-255-4	£14.99	Ipswich (pb)	1-85937-424-7	£9.99
County Durham (pb)	1-85937-398-4	£9.99	Isle of Man (pb)	1-85937-268-6	£9.99
Croydon Living Memories (pb)	1-85937-162-0	£9.99	Isle of Wight (pb)	1-85937-429-8	£9.99
Cumbria (pb)	1-85937-621-5	£9.99	Isle of Wight Living Memories	1-85937-304-6	£14.99
Derby (pb)	1-85937-367-4	£9.99	Kent (pb)	1-85937-189-2	£9.99
Derbyshire (pb)	1-85937-196-5	£9.99	Kent Living Memories(pb)	1-85937-401-8	£9.99
Derbyshire Living Memories	1-85937-330-5	£14.99	Kings Lynn (pb)	1-85937-334-8	£9.99

Available from your local bookshop or from the publisher

Frith Book Co Titles (continued)

Title	ISBN	Price	Title	ISBN	Price
Lake District (pb)	1-85937-275-9	£9.99	Sherborne (pb)	1-85937-301-1	£9.99
Lancashire Living Memories	1-85937-335-6	£14.99	Shrewsbury (pb)	1-85937-325-9	£9.99
Lancaster, Morecambe, Heysham (pb)	1-85937-233-3	£9.99	Shropshire (pb)	1-85937-326-7	£9.99
Leeds (pb)	1-85937-202-3	£9.99	Shropshire Living Memories	1-85937-643-6	£14.99
Leicester (pb)	1-85937-381-x	£9.99	Somerset	1-85937-153-1	£14.99
Leicestershire & Rutland Living Memories	1-85937-500-6	£12.99	South Devon Coast	1-85937-107-8	£14.99
Leicestershire (pb)	1-85937-185-x	£9.99	South Devon Living Memories (pb)	1-85937-609-6	£9.99
Lighthouses	1-85937-257-0	£9.99	South East London (pb)	1-85937-263-5	£9.99
Lincoln (pb)	1-85937-380-1	£9.99	South Somerset	1-85937-318-6	£14.99
Lincolnshire (pb)	1-85937-433-6	£9.99	South Wales	1-85937-519-7	£14.99
Liverpool and Merseyside (pb)	1-85937-234-1	£9.99	Southampton (pb)	1-85937-427-1	£9.99
London (pb)	1-85937-183-3	£9.99	Southend (pb)	1-85937-313-5	£9.99
London Living Memories	1-85937-454-9	£14.99	Southport (pb)	1-85937-425-5	£9.99
Ludlow (pb)	1-85937-176-0	£9.99	St Albans (pb)	1-85937-341-0	£9.99
Luton (pb)	1-85937-235-x	£9.99	St Ives (pb)	1-85937-415-8	£9.99
Maidenhead (pb)	1-85937-339-9	£9.99	Stafford Living Memories (pb)	1-85937-503-0	£9.99
Maidstone (pb)	1-85937-391-7	£9.99	Staffordshire (pb)	1-85937-308-9	£9.99
Manchester (pb)	1-85937-198-1	£9.99	Stourbridge (pb)	1-85937-530-8	£9.99
Marlborough (pb)	1-85937-336-4	£9.99	Stratford upon Avon (pb)	1-85937-388-7	£9.99
Middlesex	1-85937-158-2	£14.99	Suffolk (pb)	1-85937-221-x	£9.99
Monmouthshire	1-85937-532-4	£14.99	Suffolk Coast (pb)	1-85937-610-x	£9.99
New Forest (pb)	1-85937-390-9	£9.99	Surrey (pb)	1-85937-240-6	£9.99
Newark (pb)	1-85937-366-6	£9.99	Surrey Living Memories	1-85937-328-3	£14.99
Newport, Wales (pb)	1-85937-258-9	£9.99	Sussex (pb)	1-85937-184-1	£9.99
Newquay (pb)	1-85937-421-2	£9.99	Sutton (pb)	1-85937-337-3	£9.99
Norfolk (pb)	1-85937-195-7	£9.99	Swansea (pb)	1-85937-167-1	£9.99
Norfolk Broads	1-85937-486-7	£14.99	Taunton (pb)	1-85937-314-3	£9.99
Norfolk Living Memories (pb)	1-85937-402-6	£9.99	Tees Valley & Cleveland (pb)	1-85937-623-1	£9.99
North Buckinghamshire	1-85937-626-6	£14.99	Teignmouth (pb)	1-85937-370-4	£7.99
North Devon Living Memories	1-85937-261-9	£14.99	Thanet (pb)	1-85937-116-7	£9.99
North Hertfordshire	1-85937-547-2	£14.99	Tiverton (pb)	1-85937-178-7	£9.99
North London (pb)	1-85937-403-4	£9.99	Torbay (pb)	1-85937-597-9	£9.99
North Somerset	1-85937-302-x	£14.99	Truro (pb)	1-85937-598-7	£9.99
North Wales (pb)	1-85937-298-8	£9.99	Victorian & Edwardian Dorset	1-85937-254-6	£14.99
North Yorkshire (pb)	1-85937-236-8	£9.99	Victorian & Edwardian Kent (pb)	1-85937-624-X	£9.99
Northamptonshire Living Memories	1-85937-529-4	£14.99	Victorian & Edwardian Maritime Album (pb)	1-85937-622-3	£9.99
Northamptonshire	1-85937-150-7	£14.99	Victorian and Edwardian Sussex (pb)	1-85937-625-8	£9.99
Northumberland Tyne & Wear (pb)	1-85937-281-3	£9.99	Villages of Devon (pb)	1-85937-293-7	£9.99
Northumberland	1-85937-522-7	£14.99	Villages of Kent (pb)	1-85937-294-5	£9.99
Norwich (pb)	1-85937-194-9	£8.99	Villages of Sussex (pb)	1-85937-295-3	£9.99
Nottingham (pb)	1-85937-324-0	£9.99	Warrington (pb)	1-85937-507-3	£9.99
Nottinghamshire (pb)	1-85937-187-6	£9.99	Warwick (pb)	1-85937-518-9	£9.99
Oxford (pb)	1-85937-411-5	£9.99	Warwickshire (pb)	1-85937-203-1	£9.99
Oxfordshire (pb)	1-85937-430-1	£9.99	Welsh Castles (pb)	1-85937-322-4	£9.99
Oxfordshire Living Memories	1-85937-525-1	£14.99	West Midlands (pb)	1-85937-289-9	£9.99
Paignton (pb)	1-85937-374-7	£7.99	West Sussex (pb)	1-85937-607-x	£9.99
Peak District (pb)	1-85937-280-5	£9.99	West Yorkshire (pb)	1-85937-201-5	£9.99
Pembrokeshire	1-85937-262-7	£14.99	Weston Super Mare (pb)	1-85937-306-2	£9.99
Penzance (pb)	1-85937-595-2	£9.99	Weymouth (pb)	1-85937-209-0	£9.99
Peterborough (pb)	1-85937-219-8	£9.99	Wiltshire (pb)	1-85937-277-5	£9.99
Picturesque Harbours	1-85937-208-2	£14.99	Wiltshire Churches (pb)	1-85937-171-x	£9.99
Piers	1-85937-237-6	£17.99	Wiltshire Living Memories (pb)	1-85937-396-8	£9.99
Plymouth (pb)	1-85937-389-5	£9.99	Winchester (pb)	1-85937-428-x	£9.99
Poole & Sandbanks (pb)	1-85937-251-1	£9.99	Windsor (pb)	1-85937-333-x	£9.99
Preston (pb)	1-85937-212-0	£9.99	Wokingham & Bracknell (pb)	1-85937-329-1	£9.99
Reading (pb)	1-85937-238-4	£9.99	Woodbridge (pb)	1-85937-498-0	£9.99
Redhill to Reigate (pb)	1-85937-596-0	£9.99	Worcester (pb)	1-85937-165-5	£9.99
Ringwood (pb)	1-85937-384-4	£7.99	Worcestershire Living Memories	1-85937-489-1	£14.99
Romford (pb)	1-85937-319-4	£9.99	Worcestershire	1-85937-152-3	£14.99
Royal Tunbridge Wells (pb)	1-85937-504-9	£9.99	York (pb)	1-85937-199-x	£9.99
Salisbury (pb)	1-85937-239-2	£9.99	Yorkshire (pb)	1-85937-186-8	£9.99
Scarborough (pb)	1-85937-379-8	£9.99	Yorkshire Coastal Memories	1-85937-506-5	£14.99
Sevenoaks and Tonbridge (pb)	1-85937-392-5	£9.99	Yorkshire Dales	1-85937-502-2	£14.99
Sheffield & South Yorks (pb)	1-85937-267-8	£9.99	Yorkshire Living Memories (pb)	1-85937-397-6	£9.99

See Frith books on the internet at www.francisfrith.co.uk

FRITH PRODUCTS & SERVICES

Francis Frith would doubtless be pleased to know that the pioneering publishing venture he started in 1860 still continues today. A hundred and forty years later, The Francis Frith Collection continues in the same innovative tradition and is now one of the foremost publishers of vintage photographs in the world. Some of the current activities include:

Interior Decoration

Today Frith's photographs can be seen framed and as giant wall murals in thousands of pubs, restaurants, hotels, banks, retail stores and other public buildings throughout the country. In every case they enhance the unique local atmosphere of the places they depict and provide reminders of gentler days in an increasingly busy and frenetic world.

Product Promotions

Frith products are used by many major companies to promote the sales of their own products or to reinforce their own history and heritage. Frith promotions have been used by Hovis bread, Courage beers, Scots Porage Oats, Colman's mustard, Cadbury's foods, Mellow Birds coffee, Dunhill pipe tobacco, Guinness, and Bulmer's Cider.

Genealogy and Family History

As the interest in family history and roots grows world-wide, more and more people are turning to Frith's photographs of Great Britain for images of the towns, villages and streets where their ancestors lived; and, of course, photographs of the churches and chapels where their ancestors were christened, married and buried are an essential part of every genealogy tree and family album.

Frith Products

All Frith photographs are available Framed or just as Mounted Prints and Posters (size 23 x 16 inches). These may be ordered from the address below. From time to time other products - Address Books, Calendars, Table Mats, etc - are available.

The Internet

Already fifty thousand Frith photographs can be viewed and purchased on the internet through the Frith websites and a myriad of partner sites.

For more detailed information on Frith companies and products, look at these sites:

www.francisfrith.co.uk
www.francisfrith.com
(for North American visitors)

See the complete list of Frith Books at:

www.francisfrith.co.uk

This web site is regularly updated with the latest list of publications from the Frith Book Company. If you wish to buy books relating to another part of the country that your local bookshop does not stock, you may purchase on-line.

For further information, trade, or author enquiries please contact us at the address below:
The Francis Frith Collection, Frith's Barn, Teffont, Salisbury, Wiltshire, England SP3 5QP.
Tel: +44 (0)1722 716 376 Fax: +44 (0)1722 716 881   Email: sales@francisfrith.co.uk

See Frith books on the internet at www.francisfrith.co.uk

HOW TO ORDER YOUR FREE MOUNTED PRINT
and other Frith prints at half price

Mounted Print
Overall size 14 x 11 inches

Fill in and cut out this voucher and return it with your remittance for £2.25 (to cover postage and handling to UK addresses). For overseas addresses please include £4.00 post and handling. Choose any photograph included in this book. Your SEPIA print will be A4 in size. It will be mounted in a cream mount with a burgundy rule line (overall size 14 x 11 inches).

Order additional Mounted Prints at HALF PRICE (only £7.49 each*)
If you would like to order more Frith prints from this book, possibly as gifts for friends and family, you can buy them at half price (with no additional postage and handling costs).

Have your Mounted Prints framed
For an extra £14.95 per print* you can have your mounted print(s) framed in an elegant polished wood and gilt moulding, overall size 16 x 13 inches (no additional postage and handling required).

---

* IMPORTANT!

These special prices are only available if you order at the same time as you order your free mounted print. You must use the ORIGINAL VOUCHER on this page (no copies permitted). We can only despatch to one address.

Voucher for **FREE** and Reduced Price Frith Prints

Please do not photocopy this voucher. Only the original is valid, so please fill it in, cut it out and return it to us with your order.

Picture ref no	Page number	Qty	Mounted @ £7.49	Framed + £14.95	Total Cost
		1	Free of charge*	£	£
			£7.49	£	£
			£7.49	£	£
			£7.49	£	£
			£7.49	£	£
			£7.49	£	£
Please allow 28 days for delivery			* Post & handling (UK)		£2.25
			Total Order Cost		£

Title of this book . . . .

I enclose a cheque/postal order for £ . . . .
made payable to 'The Francis Frith Collection'

OR please debit my Mastercard / Visa / Switch / Amex card *(credit cards please on all overseas orders)*, details below

Card Number

Issue No (Switch only)   Valid from (Amex/Switch)

Expires   Signature

Name Mr/Mrs/Ms . . . .
Address . . . .
. . . .
. . . . Postcode . . . .
Daytime Tel No . . . .
Email . . . .

Valid to 31/12/05

Send completed Voucher form to:
The Francis Frith Collection, Frith's Barn, Teffont, Salisbury, Wiltshire SP3 5QP

Free Print – see overleaf

Would you like to find out more about Francis Frith?

We have recently recruited some entertaining speakers who are happy to visit local groups, clubs and societies to give an illustrated talk documenting Frith's travels and photographs. If you are a member of such a group and are interested in hosting a presentation, we would love to hear from you.

Our speakers bring with them a small selection of our local town and county books, together with sample prints. They are happy to take orders. A small proportion of the order value is donated to the group who have hosted the presentation. The talks are therefore an excellent way of fundraising for small groups and societies.

Can you help us with information about any of the Frith photographs in this book?

We are gradually compiling an historical record for each of the photographs in the Frith archive. It is always fascinating to find out the names of the people shown in the pictures, as well as insights into the shops, buildings and other features depicted.

If you recognize anyone in the photographs in this book, or if you have information not already included in the author's caption, do let us know. We would love to hear from you, and will try to publish it in future books or articles.

Our production team

Frith books are produced by a small dedicated team at offices in the converted Grade II listed 18th-century barn at Teffont near Salisbury, illustrated above. Most have worked with the Frith Collection for many years. All have in common one quality: they have a passion for the Frith Collection. The team is constantly expanding, but currently includes:

Jason Buck, John Buck, Douglas Mitchell-Burns, Ruth Butler, Heather Crisp, Isobel Hall, Julian Hight, Peter Horne, James Kinnear, Karen Kinnear, Tina Leary, David Marsh, Sue Molloy, Kate Rotondetto, Dean Scource, Eliza Sackett, Terence Sackett, Sandra Sampson, Adrian Sanders, Sandra Sanger, Julia Skinner, Lewis Taylor, Shelley Tolcher and Lorraine Tuck.